Explorers & Exploration

The Travels of
Ferdinand Magellan

By Joanne Mattern
Illustrated by Patrick O'Brien

Steadwell
Books

Raintree Steck-Vaughn Publishers
A Harcourt Company

Austin · New York
www.steck-vaughn.com

Published by Raintree Steck-Vaughn Publishers,
an imprint of Steck-Vaughn Company

Library of Congress Cataloging-in-Publication Data
Mattern, Joanne
    Ferdinand Magellan / by Joanne Mattern
      p. cm—(Explorers and exploration)
    Includes index.
    Summary: Presents a biography of the Portuguese sea captain who commanded the first expedition that sailed around the world.
    ISBN 0-7398-1484-2
      1. Magalhäes, Fernäo de, d. 1521—Juvenile literature.
2. Explorers—Portugal—Biography—Juvenile literature. 3. Voyages around the world—Juvenile literature. [1. Magellan, Ferdinand, d. 1521. 2. Explorers. 3. Voyages around the world.] I. Title. II. Series.

G286.M2 M38 2000
910.4'1—dc21   99-055480

Printed in the United States of America
10 9 8 7 6 5 4 3 2 1 LB 02 01 00 99

Produced by By George Productions, Inc.

Illustration Acknowledgments:
P. 5, North Wind Pictures; pp. 9, 37, 39, John Blazejewski; pp. 5, 21, 32, 34, 35, 40, The New York Public Library Picture Collection; p. 23, The New York Historical Society; pp. 24–25, Stock Montage; p. 26, Courtesy of the John Carter Brown Library at Brown University.
All other artwork is by Patrick O'Brien.

Contents

Soldier and Sailor

If you looked at a map of the world in 1480, it would look very different from a map of today. The continents of Europe, Asia, and Africa would be on the map. But North and South America would not be, because Europeans did not know they existed. Instead, an ocean stretched across the bottom of the world, with no continents to separate its waters.

Ferdinand Magellan was born around 1480 in Portugal. His adventures would change the map of the world forever.

Ferdinand was born into a wealthy family. His father was the mayor of the town where the Magellans lived. When he was a boy, Ferdinand was sent to the court of King John II of Portugal to serve as a page. Pages were young boys who did tasks for members of the royal court. In return they received an education.

Ferdinand studied arithmetic, science, and music. Because King John was interested in exploration, Ferdinand's lessons also included geography and navigation. Navigation means using maps and instruments to find your way. Ferdinand dreamed of going to sea someday.

A map of the world made about 1492

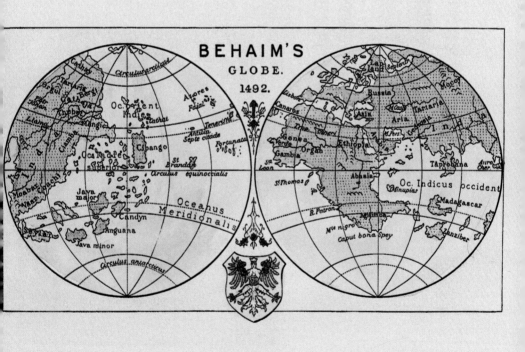

Navigators from Magellan's time did not have good maps to guide them. Instead, they used devices like this hourglass and traverse board.

In the 16th century, Portugal was a very powerful country. Portugal and its enemy, Spain, traded with the Far East for spices, fine silks, and jewels. The Far East is made up of the countries of eastern Asia—China, Japan, Korea, and Mongolia. But the trip by ship to Asia was not an easy one. A ship had to make a long journey around Africa. Explorers were always looking for new and better ways to get to the Far East.

In 1505, when Magellan was about 25 years old, he finally got the chance to go to sea. King John II had died, and his brother-in-law, Manuel, became king. King Manuel sent a fleet of ships to India. Magellan signed up for the voyage as a sailor.

The next year Magellan went on a trip to Africa. The king wanted to keep Arab traders away from the African coast so that Portugal could build its own trading posts there.

In 1507 Magellan returned to India. While he was there, he fought in many battles against the Arabs. His bravery earned him a higher rank. Soon he was no longer just a sailor but a ship's officer.

In 1511 Magellan helped Portugal gain control of a group of islands below India, in the Indian Ocean. Today they are known as Indonesia. Many of these islands were so rich in spices they were called the Spice Islands. Now they are known as the Moluccas.

Some of the other sailors became jealous of Magellan. In 1513 they made up charges against him. They convinced the captain of the fleet to send Magellan back to Portugal in disgrace.

Magellan also got into trouble because of a report he wrote. In 1494, Spain and Portugal drew up the Treaty of Tordesillas. As a result of this treaty, an imaginary line was drawn from the north to the south on the globe. All the land the explorers reached that was west of this line belonged to Spain. All the land east of the line belonged to Portugal. While Magellan was in the Far East, he studied a map of the world. When he saw where the Spice Islands were located, he realized that they actually belonged to Spain. King Manuel and the other Portuguese officials were angry. There was no way that they would let these islands belong to another country.

Magellan did not stay in Portugal for long. Fighting broke out between the Portuguese and a group of native people called the Moors in the northern African country of Morocco. King Manuel sent Magellan to war. His knee was badly injured during one of the battles. For the rest of his life, Magellan walked with a limp.

A portrait of Ferdinand Magellan

Magellan's bad luck continued. While he was guarding some animals captured from the Moors, several of them disappeared. He was charged with selling the animals back to the Moors and keeping the money for himself. Although Magellan was later cleared of all charges, he once again returned to Portugal in disgrace.

An Amazing Dream

When Magellan returned to Portugal in 1514, he was tired of fighting battles. He was also tired of being under the command of other men. He wanted to explore the world as captain of his own ship.

Magellan had studied the trips of other explorers. Almost all of them had reached the Far East by sailing east. Magellan thought there might be a better way. He wanted to sail west and circumnavigate, or go around, the world.

Magellan went to King Manuel and described his plan. But the king did not like or trust Magellan. This was because of the trouble Magellan had had in the past. King Manuel refused to go along with Magellan's plan.

Sailors on ships often climbed ropes to sight land.

MAGELLAN'S ROUTE AROUND THE WORLD

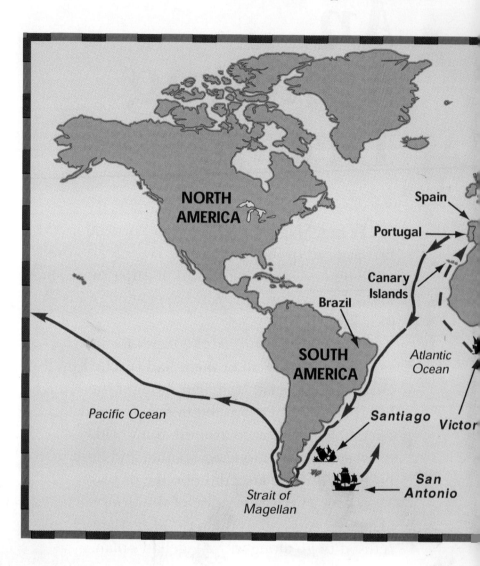

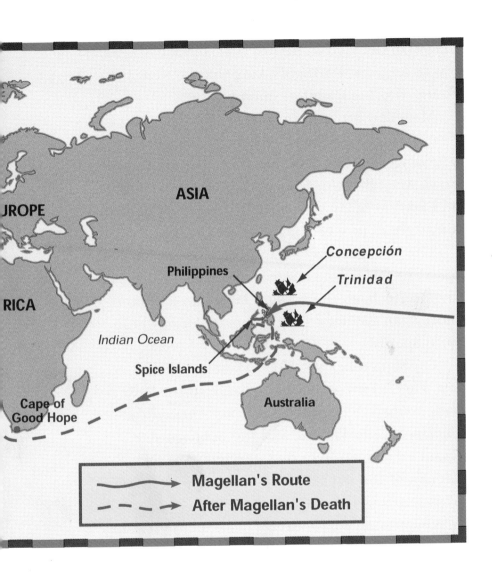

EUROPE

ASIA

AFRICA

Philippines

Concepción

Trinidad

Indian Ocean

Spice Islands

Cape of
Good Hope

Australia

→ Magellan's Route

--→ After Magellan's Death

Magellan was angry. The king then told him he was free to take his plan to another country. Magellan decided to do just that. In fact, Magellan was so angry at Portugal's king that he went to Spain—Portugal's bitter enemy.

Magellan brought his plan to King Charles I of Spain. The king knew about Magellan's bravery. The king liked the fact that Portugal had turned down Magellan. And King Charles also wanted to add land to Spain's empire. In 1518 the Spanish king agreed to send Magellan on his trip.

The king gave Magellan five ships and money for a crew. He also promised Magellan a share in any profits from the voyage. Magellan gathered more than 250 men for the trip, most of whom were Spanish.

On September 20, 1519, Magellan set out at last. He had five galleons, or large ships. They were named the *Trinidad,* the *San Antonio,* the *Concepción,* the *Victoria,* and the *Santiago.* A Spaniard named Juan de Cartagena was the captain of the largest of the ships, the *San Antonio.* This ship was about 150 feet (45 m) long. Magellan was captain of the second-largest ship, the *Trinidad.*

One of Magellan's ships, the *Victoria*

From the beginning of the voyage, there were problems. The ships were crowded. There were rats and lice. The food was salted meat, cheese, and hard biscuits. On a long voyage, these foods spoiled before the journey's end. Because the men had no fruit or vegetables to eat, many became sick with a disease called scurvy. This disease is caused by a lack of vitamin C, which is found in fruits and vegetables.

But the biggest problem Magellan had was with his crew. Because Spain and Portugal were such bitter enemies, the Spanish crew did not trust the Portuguese Magellan. Worst of all, Magellan and Cartagena, the Spanish captain of the *San Antonio*, did not get along.

Ferdinand Magellan on board one of his ships

Troubles and Triumphs

Seven days after they left Spain, Magellan and his ships arrived in the Canary Islands off the northwest coast of Africa. After a quick stop for fresh food and water, the ships set off down the coast of Africa. Here the first major quarrel between Magellan and Cartagena started. Cartagena thought Magellan was sticking too close to the coast. He wanted to set out across the Atlantic. Cartagena spoke rudely to Magellan. Furious, Magellan arrested Cartagena and took him aboard the *Victoria* as a prisoner. Magellan had won this argument. But the other Spanish captains now had even more reason not to like or trust him.

At last the fleet turned west across the Atlantic. The weather was bad. Fierce storms battered the ships. Then the ships sailed into the doldrums. This is a place near the equator where there is almost no wind. The ships sat without moving in

18 ～～

the middle of the ocean for more than three weeks. The hot sun blazed down, melting the tar in the ships' timbers. This caused the ships to leak. Water barrels broke and the food spoiled even more quickly in the heat.

At last the ocean currents pushed the ships north, out of the doldrums. The sails filled with wind, and the ships were once more on their way.

In early December 1519, Magellan and his crew reached Brazil. This is a very big country on the continent of South America. The ships anchored in the harbor of what is now Rio de Janeiro. The crew was happy to be there. They got busy repairing the ships and loading fresh food and water. They also made friends and traded with the native people.

Birds like this one often came on board when Magellan's ships neared land.

Brazil was part of Portugal's empire. But the Portuguese had not made many settlements in this rich and large country. This was lucky for Magellan. He could go ashore. He could trade with the native people without fear of being caught by the Portuguese for being on their land.

Magellan and his crew rested for two weeks. Then they began the next part of their trip on the morning of December 25. They sailed down the coast of South America. They were looking for a strait, or narrow passage of water. They hoped this would lead across the continent and into another ocean in the west. They passed several places, but none of them led to the ocean.

Magellan's biggest problem was that he had no maps or charts to guide him. This is because no European had ever sailed around South America. Magellan had no idea if the strait he was looking for was even there. But he was sure he would find a passage to the western ocean. So he sailed on.

The farther south the ships sailed, the colder the weather became. As they sailed close to Antarctica and the South Pole, freezing winds ripped across the decks. Sleet and snow chilled the men, who did not have warm clothes for this kind of weather. Icebergs drifted by, threatening to crush the ships. The men kept from starving by killing and eating penguins. Even so they were terribly hungry.

Near Antarctica and the South Pole, Magellan's crew had to eat penguins to keep from starving.

Magellan knew they had to find a place to wait out the cold weather. On March 31, 1520, the ships sailed into a bay on the coast of what is now Argentina. The men met some native people. They were all about 7 feet (2.1 m) tall! But then a fight broke out. One of the Spanish sailors and several of the native people were killed.

Magellan soon had other problems. Juan de Cartagena escaped from his prison aboard the *Victoria*. He convinced several of the sailors on the *Concepción* to mutiny against Magellan. A mutiny happens when a crew goes against the ship's captain. Cartagena wanted to name himself the leader.

The mutineers easily captured the *San Antonio*. Some men aboard the *Victoria*, the *Concepción*, and the *San Antonio* began to cheer. "Death to Magellan! Long live Cartagena!" they shouted.

Magellan responded quickly to the attack. He sent men from the *Trinidad* and the *Santiago* against the mutineers. The mutineers were frightened when they saw the armed sailors coming. Magellan and his men captured the *Victoria* and threatened to shoot at the mutineers' two remaining ships with cannons. The mutineers gave up.

This picture shows Magellan as he nears the coast of South America.

Magellan allowed most of the mutineers to go free. But he had harsh punishment for their leaders. The captain of the *Concepción* was put to death. Cartagena and a priest who was his friend were left on a desert island and never heard from again.

Not long after that the *Santiago* was smashed during a storm. But although he had only four ships left, Magellan sailed on.

In October 1520 another storm forced the ships into a bay. When the storm ended, Magellan knew that the wind and waves had carried them into deep water. Magellan wanted to explore where this led. On October 21, 1520, Magellan and his men found a narrow opening between the land. Magellan was sure they had at last discovered a passage around South America.

A painting of the discovery of the deep-water passageway that led Magellan to the Pacific Ocean

This map from the 16th century shows Magellan's route around the world. The place names are written in Latin.

It took five long weeks to sail through the narrow strait, which is now called the Strait of Magellan. The weather was cold and stormy, and many of the men wanted to give up. One night the *San Antonio* and its crew slipped away and sailed back to Spain. But Magellan sailed on.

On November 28, 1520, the ships sailed out of the strait and into the ocean. When Magellan saw the ocean, he wept tears of joy. Then he called his men together and named the ocean *Mar Pacifico*—"Peaceful Sea." Today this body of water is known as the Pacific Ocean.

The crew of the *San Antonio* sailed back to Spain in the middle of the night.

A Bitter Ending

Magellan had no idea how large the Pacific Ocean is. He thought the ships would reach the Spice Islands in just a few days. But weeks, then months, passed with no sign of land. Once again the men suffered from hunger and thirst. Their food spoiled quickly under the hot sun. One sailor wrote in his diary, "We ate biscuit which was no longer biscuit, but powder of biscuit swarming with worms." The hungry men ate anything they could find—even rats, insects, and sawdust. Many of the men became ill with scurvy. Sores covered their skin, and their arms and legs became swollen. Nineteen men died.

At last, on March 7, 1521, the ships reached the island that is now called Guam. Magellan and his crew had sailed more than 8,000 miles (12,900 km) of ocean!

Magellan hoped to land on the island and get a new supply of fresh food and water. But the natives stole the small boat that had carried Magellan's men to shore. A fierce battle followed, and Magellan was forced to leave the island.

Ten days later the ships reached the islands that are now the Philippines. Here the people were friendly. Magellan claimed the islands for Spain.

Sometimes on board Magellan's ships the crew had to eat anything they could find, even if it was rotten.

Victoria

Though Magellan was interested in getting to the Spice Islands, he also had another aim. He wanted to convert the native people to Christianity. He and his men traveled to many of the islands and had great success. On the island of Cebu, Magellan held a huge ceremony. The ruler of the island, his family, and hundreds of his subjects were baptized as Christians.

Next Magellan moved on to the island of Mactan. But the people there were not as friendly. Nor did they want to become Christians. Magellan and 60 of his men landed on Mactan on April 27, 1521. They were met by a thousand unfriendly natives.

Most of the sailors escaped back to the ships. But Magellan was struck by spears and was killed. Magellan's men offered to buy back his body, but the native leader refused. The crew finally left without Magellan's body.

A drawing that shows the battles Magellan faced in the Philippines

Magellan was killed in battle on the island of Mactan, in the Philippines.

Heading Home

After Magellan's death the Spanish captains decided to continue the journey. Because there were not enough men to sail three ships, they sank the *Concepción*. The *Trinidad* and the *Victoria* set off for the Spice Islands. They reached the islands in November 1521—after more than two years at sea!

Although the Spice Islands belonged to Portugal, the native people were eager to trade with the Spanish crewmen. There was no trouble, so Magellan's crew stayed on the islands for almost three months. Finally, in February 1522, the two remaining ships were filled with precious goods. The men headed west across the Indian Ocean, toward home.

It was not long before disaster struck. The *Trinidad* was so overloaded that it began to leak. Rather than leave the ship, its crew decided to sail back across the Pacific to South America. They thought this would be an easier route than following the *Victoria* around India and Africa.

Magellan's crew reached the Spice Islands after more than two years at sea

The route the *Trinidad* took turned out to be a bad idea. The wind was against them, and the captain finally turned back toward the Spice Islands. This time they landed on an island where there were Portuguese. The entire crew was taken by the Portuguese and put into prison. The Portuguese said that the Spanish had no right to be in the Spice Islands, since these islands belonged to Portugal.

Some members of the *Trinidad*'s crew died in prison. A few chose to remain on the islands after their release. Only four members of the crew finally returned to Spain. Experts are not sure what happened to the *Trinidad*. The Portuguese might have destroyed it, or the leaky ship may have sunk.

The *Victoria*, with Juan Sebastián del Cano as captain, sailed across the Indian Ocean. Del Cano chose a long, difficult route in order to avoid Portuguese-held islands. He told his men that death was better than a Portuguese prison. The men agreed, even though they suffered terribly from hunger and disease.

The *Victoria* sailed across the southern tip of Africa and around the Cape of Good Hope. Then the ship traveled up the western coast of Africa until it reached the Cape Verde Islands. These islands were held by Portugal, but del Cano's men

Juan Sebastián del Cano sailed the *Victoria* back to Spain.

were so weak and sick that he had to risk stopping there for food and water.

Del Cano told the Portuguese officials that he had been sailing in Spanish waters. But the Portuguese soon found out that the *Victoria* was carrying goods from the Spice Islands. Del Cano went back to his ship and left the islands. Several sailors who were ashore were not able to escape. They were arrested by the Portuguese.

A 1603 German navigation book included this map of the Strait of Magellan.

September 8, 1522, was a day del Cano and his men would never forget. On that day they sailed into the Spanish harbor of Sanlúcar de Barrameda. Three years before, five ships and more than 250 men had left that harbor on their amazing voyage. Only one ship and 18 men returned.

Although Magellan did not live to complete his voyage, his dream had come true. His ship, the *Victoria*, had circled the globe.

Magellan also discovered a strait in South America that made it possible for ships to sail from the Atlantic Ocean to the Pacific Ocean. The passageway is now called the Strait of Magellan. This important discovery opened up even more trade for Europe. And Magellan himself lives on in history as one of the world's greatest navigators and explorers.

Other Events of the 16th Century
(1501 – 1600)

During the century that Magellan was sailing, events were happening in other parts of the world. Some of these were:

1502   Portuguese navigator Vasco da Gama makes his second voyage to India in order to expand trade.

1521   Hernán Cortés, a Spanish conquistador, conquers the Aztec Empire in Mexico.

1524   Giovanni da Verrazano, an Italian sailor, explores the coast of North America from North Carolina to Maine.

1534   Francisco Pizarro of Spain conquers the Inca Empire in Peru.

1571   Portuguese create colony in Angola, Africa.

1578   Moroccans destroy Portuguese power in northwest Africa.

Time Line

1480 (?)	Ferdinand Magellan is born to a wealthy family in Portugal.
1493 (?)	Magellan becomes a page in the court of King John II, where he learns geography and navigation.
1505	Magellan sails to India as part of a Portuguese fleet.
1512	Magellan is injured in a battle in Morocco.
1516	Magellan presents his idea of circling the globe to King Manuel of Portugal and is refused. Magellan takes his idea to Spain.
1518	King Charles I of Spain pays for Magellan's journey and gives him five ships.
September 20, 1519	Magellan and his ships set sail for the Far East.
March 31, 1520	Magellan and his crew spend the winter in the Bay of San Julian, in what is now Argentina.

October 21, 1520	Magellan discovers a passageway across South America, now known as the Strait of Magellan.
November 28, 1520	The fleet reaches the Pacific Ocean.
March 7, 1521	Magellan reaches Guam.
March-April, 1521	Magellan and his men travel around the Philippines, converting many native people to Christianity.
April 27, 1521	Magellan is killed on the Philippine island of Mactan.
September 8, 1522	The *Victoria* and 18 men return to Spain, completing the first circumnavigation of the world.

Glossary

bay A part of the ocean that is partly enclosed by land

Canary Islands Islands in the Atlantic Ocean off the northwest coast of Africa

Cebu (say-BOO) An island in the central Philippines

Christianity (kris-chee-AN-uh-tee) The religion that is based on the teachings of Jesus Christ and uses the Bible as holy scripture

circumnavigate (sur-kum-NAV-uh-gate) To travel all the way around the world

convert (kun-VERT) To change from one belief to another

de Cartagena, Juan (day kart-a-HAY-nah, WAN) The Spanish captain of the *San Antonio*

del Cano, Juan Sebastián (del KAN-o, WAN suh-BAS-ti-an) The captain of the *Victoria* on the journey back from the Philippines

doldrums (DOLE-drumz) Areas of the ocean near the equator where there is almost no wind and the sea is very calm

equator (ih-KWAY-tur) An imaginary circle around Earth, halfway between the North Pole and the South Pole

Far East The countries of East Asia, including China, Japan, Korea, and Mongolia. Sometimes the term includes the countries of Southeast Asia and the Malay Archipelago

galleon (GAL-ee-uhn) A large sailing ship used from the 15th to the 18th centuries for trading and warfare

harbor (HAR-bur) A place where ships can anchor safely

Mactan (mak-TAN) An island in the central Philippines

Moors (MOORZ) Nomadic people of northern Africa who spread into Spain and conquered most of the country in the 8th century

mutineer (mute-uh-NEER) A person who takes part in a mutiny

mutiny (MUTE-uh-nee) A rebellion in which sailors refuse to obey their captain and take control of the ship

navigation (NAV-uh-gay-shun) Traveling with the use of maps and instruments to find the way

page (PAYJ) A boy who served in the royal court and received an education there

Rio de Janeiro (REE-oh day JAN-ehr-oh) A port in Brazil

Sanlúcar de Barrameda (SAN LUK-ar day bah-rah-MAY-da) The Spanish harbor into which the *Victoria* arrived more than two years after its departure

scurvy (SKER-vee) A disease caused by a lack of vitamin C

strait (strayt) A narrow waterway that connects two larger bodies of water

Treaty of Tordesillas (TREET-ee of tor-duh-SEE-yahs) An agreement between Spain and Portugal that divided the recently reached lands between the two countries

Index